A Faith That Works

Moving From Seeing To Believing

Teresa A. Stith

A FAITH THAT WORKS

Copyright © 2018- Teresa A. Stith

All rights reserved. This book is protected by the copyright laws of the United States of America. This book may not be copied or reprinted for commercial gain or profit. The use of short quotations or occasional page copying for personal or group study is permitted and encouraged. Permission will be granted upon request.

Unless otherwise identified, scripture quotations are from the King James version of the Bible. Copyright © 1982 by Thomas Nelson, Inc. Used by permission. All rights reserved.

Please note that certain pronouns referring to the Father, Son, and the Holy Spirit may be capitalized to acknowledge Him as Creator and any other such titles. Please note also that the name satan and related names are not capitalized. We choose not to acknowledge him, even to the point of violating grammatical rules.

Cover Design: Jessica David

ISBN-13: 978-0692111499

ISBN-10: 0692111492

Publisher- Teresa A. Stith

Printing Company- CreateSpace

Website: afaiththatworks.com

A Faith That Works

Moving From Seeing To Believing

"For we are saved by hope:
but hope that is seen is not hope:
for what a man seeth,
why doth he yet hope for?"
(Romans 8:24)

"And blessed is she who believes

that the Lord shall fulfill

His promises to her:

for there shall be a performance

of those things which were told her

from the Lord" (Luke 1:45)

DEDICATION

This book is FIRST dedicated to God, My Lord and Savior Jesus Christ, and the residing presence of the Holy Ghost who, only by His inspiration and ultimate design, am I able to discover the hidden truths of His Word and the talents and abilities that laid dormant in my life for so long. To my Pastor Dennis C. Ruffin and in memory of my First Lady, the late Dr. Miranda T. Ruffin (1955-2016) who took me wholeheartedly into their lives and practically raised me as one of their own. Laboring tirelessly with me, that I might come to know Jesus Christ as my own personal Lord and Savior. Whom God allowed (by His Holy Spirit) to chase after me because He had a greater purpose for my life than what I was able to see at the time. They preached, taught, sacrificed, and chastised me spiritually that I might discover my full potential in God. That I might be equipped to teach others and draw them to the foot of the Cross. Their labor of love will never be forgotten. It was an honor to sit at their feet and feast from their table of wisdom, knowledge, and understanding. I strive daily to serve God with ALL my strength and all diligence of Spirit that I will be found in peace by Him at the day of His return.

To the Women of Strength, my Sisters in Christ, who fought the good fight of faith with me. We've toiled, we've labored, we've cried, we've stumbled, and we've failed. So many times we've felt like giving up, BUT we pushed onward. We fought each other through our ignorance of the Word, our selfishness, our lack of understanding, our differences, and our refusal to face our worse enemy…OURSELVES!!! Holding on to the Promise, we each have discovered her true nature of praise and worship to Our Lord through songs, testimonies, and manifestations of spiritual blessings of love, joy, peace, and unity. Before we could serve others, we had to first learn to serve one another.

What a joy it has been to serve you, My Sisters.

Table of Contents

Chapter 1: When Faith Didn't Work 1

Chapter 2 : Overcoming Obstacles 25

Chapter 3: Losing Myself 37

Chapter 4: Deciding To Trust 49

Chapter 5: Accountability 63

Faith In Action 71

Bonus: My Testimony 75

My Message To You 79

Sorrow Turned Into Joy 83

About The Author 85

Do not love the world or anything in the world. If anyone loves the world, love for the Father is not in them. For everything in the world-the lust of the flesh, the lust of the eyes, and the pride of life-comes not from the Father but from the world. The world and its desires pass away, but whoever does the will of God lives forever.

1 John 2: 15-17 (NIV)

PREFACE

Humility is one of the greatest lessons I've had to learn on this journey, for it has allowed me to be broken in areas of my life where I sought the most control. Losing control made me feel vulnerable in some areas, and like a failure in others. Little did I know that these moments would be the highlights of my life because they would produce a strength in me that I did not even know existed. They taught me how to hold fast to my faith and trust God even when I could not see (with natural eyes) Him at work behind the scenes on my behalf. Trusting God with the measure of faith that He has given me, taught me how to be effective in leading others to Christ by sharing with them my experiences. Teaching them to wait on the Lord with all diligence and with joy realizing that…He is not unrighteous to forget your work and labour of love, which ye have shewed toward His name, in that ye have ministered to the saints, and do minister (Hebrews 6:10, KJV).

"A Faith That Works" was written to encourage, motivate, and build you up in the area of your faith. I have a strong compassion and love for people that when they are sad, troubled, discouraged, depressed, feeling unloved or rejected, I pick up on it and I go to them and give them a word of hope. I am reminded how the Spirit of the Lord led Ezekiel in the middle of a valley filled with dry bones. He asked Ezekiel "Son of man can these bones live?" Ezekiel said "O Sovereign Lord, you alone know." Then He said to Ezekiel, "Prophesy to these bones and say to them, 'Dry bones, hear the word of the Lord!" This is what the Sovereign Lord says to these bones: I will make breath enter you, and you will come to life (Ezekiel 3: 3-5).

I look for opportunities to speak life into someone else. Someone who is lost on this journey or someone who has given up on life. Someone who cannot see pass the "right now". God's Spirit in me allows me to connect with these people to restore the joy in them that they once knew.

Writing this book has caused me to excel and exceed my own expectations!!! See I was a wretch undone, had no hope of ever doing anything great in my life. Never thought I was good enough and looking for love in all the wrong places. I considered myself a failure until the Lord revealed how fearfully and wonderfully made He had created me to be. I will bless the Lord every day of my life for His grace and mercy. I know who I am and WHOSE I AM. It is this priority of keeping "First Things First" that I have embraced and now walk in this NEWNESS!!! I know a MAN that inspite of my circumstances and all of the emotional scars, suicidal thoughts, depression, and rejection, specialized in turning my whole life around. I am a witness of God's goodness to me in the land of the living. Reading this book drove me to tears as I recall each stage in the process of my own development. I will tell you that I now cry tears of joy to discover that God was with me all along working things out, loving me through my messes and strengthening me for this Greater Purpose. Wherever you are on your journey, DON'T QUIT!!! What you are experiencing may not feel good, but God is working it all out for your good. Plant your feet and stay the course!!!

"But as it is written,

Eye hath not seen, nor ear heard,
neither have entered into the heart of man,
the things which God hath prepared

for them that love Him"

(1 Cor. 2:9)

INTRODUCTION

"*A* Faith That Works" is very motivational and written to help you overcome your own obstacles and use the mustard seed measure of faith that has already been given to you to receive God's best for your life. Journey with me as you discover new heights and deeper depths to your faith which lies IN YOU. We can be our worst enemy when it comes to using our faith to receive from God. Let Him stretch you, let Him make you uncomfortable as you grow in grace and in the knowledge of our Lord and Savior Jesus Christ. Faith does not work according to how we feel, or what we think, but according to how we believe.

"*A* Faith That Works" will help you discover the TRUTH about God and His undying love for us, even in our ignorance of who He is. You will also learn to be accountable by surrendering "Your Will" to God and making an honest effort to trust Him in every area of your life. Get ready to be "BROKEN". The Bible tells us in Matthew 16:25, "For whosoever will save his life shall lose it: and whosoever will lose his life for My sake shall find it. Maybe some of the things that have come to test my faith has tried to test yours too. Let

"A Faith That Works" challenge you to search your inner self and discover truths about your own self and your own faith that will move you toward an even closer and more personal relationship with the Lord. Let the love of God draw you into divine fellowship with Him. Do not be afraid of what God will show you about yourself in these pages, for this is the beginning of the transformation process. We hope that this book allows you to begin that process with all readiness of Spirit and with a genuine desire for change. If you are ready…READ ON!!!

CHAPTER 1

WHEN FAITH DIDN'T WORK

The bible tells us in Hebrews 11:1 "NOW faith is the substance of things hoped for, the evidence of things not seen". "For in this hope we were saved. But hope that is seen is no hope at all. Who hopes for what they already have?" (Rom. 8:24, NIV). Faith is the confidence that what we hope for will actually happen; it gives us assurance about things we cannot physically see (Heb. 11:1, NLT).

You are probably saying that "this doesn't make sense" and "who has ever known faith not to work?" Well…you are correct. In me, the issue was not with the faith at all, the issue was with my ability to believe God inspite of my circumstances. I was operating based on what I was seeing rather than what God had said. Was I worthy to receive anything from Him? Why was He always so mindful of me? I had a hard time trying to figure out why I felt so differently from other people. I often battled whether or not I was liked by others and felt that I was probably better off dead. But something kept moving in me. I did not know at this time that it was God because my circumstances blinded me to anything related to whether God even existed. In this place there was peace though, a peace that I only felt when I came back to this place. Whatever this was, it just kept pulling on me!!! Let's talk about my plights.

Growing up I yearned to be loved. I cannot recall when I began to experience these feelings but they haunted my life throughout my childhood and as a young adult. I just couldn't understand why no one liked me. I was not liked in school, I didn't feel like I was liked at home most times, and I always asked myself why. Why did I feel so different? I knew that there was something strange about me, but I did not know what it was, I blamed myself for my bad life and eventually learned to accept it. I remember always trying to make myself fit, always trying to be noticed. I would jump in other people's conversations or strike up conversations with strangers all in an effort to fill this lonely void that was taking a deep seeded root in my heart. People made me feel that I was unworthy, that I wasn't good enough and I believed them after a while. I felt that I could not accomplish anything. I thought that my dark-skin made me ugly and I hated myself for being dark. I argued with God about why He did not make me light and pretty with a different name and at times, with a different family. We were always struggling. I just wanted to be accepted. I wanted someone to care about what I was experiencing. I wanted a different life.

I remember overhearing one of my cousins on the phone talking to a young man that I told her I liked. She knew him very well because they went to school together so she called him in an effort to get us together. She was trying her best to describe me to him. I finally heard him say "oh, oh she has short hair?" I heard my cousin say yes, and he boldly stated "man she is black as ---!!!" I never told my cousin that I heard the conversation but those words were only another tactic that satan used to keep me in bondage. That seed along with many others was planted in my mind and took an even deeper root in my heart. The thought that no one would ever want me because I was black and ugly began to take its toll on how and what I did from that point forward. I had not learned yet how to lift myself out of this place so I began to sink, spiraling down into a state of depression.

"For You formed my inward parts; You wove me in my mother's womb. I will give thanks to You, for I am fearfully and wonderfully made; Wonderful are Your works, and my soul knows

it very well. My frame was not hidden from You when I was made in secret, and skillfully wrought in the depths of the earth"
(Psa. 134: 14-15, NASB)

You are not a mistake!!! I do not care when you arrived on the scene or how, you are NOT a mistake. God has a divine plan for ALL of us. We all have unique features, gifts, and callings that separates us from one another. God praised His own work when He looked at us and saw that what He had made was very good!!! Nothing about my life, my journey, or my path has been hidden from Him. He has seen every tear, every heartache, every hurt, every imperfection, every struggle, and every sin, and has loved me no less. He has predestined me, called me, justified me, and when this life is over, He will glorify me. The bible says "What then shall we say in response to these things? If God is for us, who can be against us?" (Rom. 8:30, Berean Study Bible).

*B*UT…I was already broken when I came to the Lord as a young girl looking for meaning and answers to the already chaotic life that I was living. A seed of bitterness had already been rooted in me and I was so lost. It was hard for me to comprehend things that normal people knew already like simple table manners. I felt stupid, like it was a challenge for me to understand certain things. Being around certain people made me inferior to them. I felt less than the least of all people. My self-esteem was shot, blown out like a fuse. I always felt like I was being watched so I was careful not to mess up but I failed anyway. I could not seem to do anything right. I knew that I wanted better for my life and I was determined to have better, but I felt that people expected me to lose, so winning for me was out of the question. I became a person that everyone else wanted me to be and lost my own identity in the process. I was a yes person afraid to tell anybody no because I did not want to be alone. Although people made me feel unworthy I felt that they still somehow validated me. I needed their opinions of me even when it hurt.

I had little knowledge about who God was during this time and no clue as to the power that He possessed to totally transform my life. I was living at only 19 years old, what I believed to be my last days. My life was so bad (I thought) that surely I would not live too much longer!!! Things could not get any worse than what they were at this moment. I was mentally oppressed and depressed and did not want to go on living. Nothing at this point in my life seemed to be working or making any sense but I thought this was how life was supposed to be because I had allowed myself to conform to this way of thinking. I could not see pass my present state to believe God for greater. I was a single mom with a two year old, relationship issues, pregnant with my second child, no job, no money, no transportation and feeling isolated like the "black sheep" of my family. I was so depressed. I would wake up and go back to sleep, seeing no need to get up and face another dreadful day. I would not even comb my hair, there was no justifiable reason to because I was dying inside. I remember when I graduated from high school, it should have been one of the happiest days of my life, but it wasn't. I will never forget how much it bothered me to graduate. Although I was truly grateful that I had made my grade and graduated, I was not ready to stop going to school. I loved school. School helped me to escape the loneliness I felt when I was home. Whenever it snowed, I was pitiful because school would be closed. I knew I would be in the house all day and I would much rather have been learning. If we were at school and had to leave early, I would cry inside. The other kids would be cheering because they were excited about going home but I wondered "why would they be so happy to go home?" I figured that surely there was something going on in their home that was not taking place in mine, but I kept my thoughts to myself. I never talked a lot about my feelings, I expressed them in other ways. I acted out.

I had no sense of direction and nowhere to go when I left school (no real purpose in life). I had never had a job of any kind, no more than the summer school program so I didn't even have skills to get a job. My mother and father had separated prior to my graduation and dad had custody of myself and other siblings. There wasn't a lot of teaching, training, or structure on how to live life because he was obviously very busy doing his own thing. We had to pretty much figure life out on our own. Myself, and two older brothers struggled to provide for ourselves and younger siblings but I think that God was somewhere close by because things always came together. I did not know this for sure because I hadn't come to know Him fully yet.

My mom was awarded full custody of us eventually and she remarried. Soon after, my father would go on to be with the Lord. He left this world two weeks before I had my first child (his first grandchild). His death took a great toll on me. I wanted to be where my father was, I missed him. But even in the midst of all of this chaos and emotion, I sought a "Higher Power". I began to read my Bible. Still not knowing what faith really was, God kept me and sustained me and I had hope for better days. So you see, faith is something that you use unconsciously. It is "just knowing" or "believing" that something is going to happen because of what you are doing to make it happen!!! "Faith without works is dead" (James 2: 14-26).

Although I had my struggles with wanting to be loved, understanding life and my own purpose for living, I wanted to give love as well. I knew that love filled my heart because I could feel it, I just didn't understand it. I loved people!!! It felt like an overflowing cup sitting in my chest where my heart is, just waiting to be emptied or poured into someone else's life. Because of a lack of understanding surrounding "how to love" it was often misused and taken advantage of. I remember crying and asking one of my friends "why people hearts are not like mine?" "Why people do not love like I do?" My friend explained to me that in this life you will come across a lot of people whose only motive is to use and abuse others, "but" she said, "you keep being you, keep loving others and God will reward you one day". So as young as I was, I not only struggled with these issues of life, I struggled to understand this love in my heart and why it was so consistently being trampled upon. I needed to understand Him. No matter how hard I tried to make people love me back, it seemed that they disliked me more. Have you ever had someone to dislike you for no justifiable reason at all? I realized later that the only reason I was able to embrace these people and connect or identify so strongly with them was because they were broken too, and just like me they were wanting to be accepted and loved as well.

I felt like the whole world was against me!!! I began to become very promiscuous, I thought this was love. At least I got the attention that I so desperately longed for, if only for a moment. I was so naïve. I was grown but uneducated when it came to how I should conduct myself around men. I wanted something that I felt only they could provide and I found myself falling significantly for one after the other. The relationships would only last for a little while, but then I was right back to square one....ALL ALONE, BY MYSELF. I began to feel like something was wrong with me. I'd never had a steady friend or anyone that I could call "mine". My father had passed, and I did not have a close relationship with my brothers. I cried all the time asking God why had my life been so complicated? What was wrong with me? I began to LOOK at myself and I SAW everything that was wrong with me, why nobody wanted me....ALL I WANTED WAS LOVE!!! That was my desire, my drive, my passion, my focus, my motivation. I had such a strong yearning in my heart for LOVE. 💕

Since writing this book, I have gone back and checked some things, remembered some things, and accepted some things about my past. I've had to let go of some things as well. I do not have the power to turn back the hands of time, but I can surely lay hold of the future by releasing all of the pains of my childhood experiences and trading them for joy and freedom in Christ Jesus who through faith has liberated me high above my tests and trials. Recalling the events that took place in my life so long ago helped me to find clarity in this present life that I now live.

When I went back and looked closely at my father, I can picture this one episode. He's sitting on the edge of the bed and he's looking at me. He has asked me to do something (maybe bring him a glass of water) and he's watching me as I follow his instructions. My dad made me feel so nervous I don't know why. I loved my father so much, but I was afraid to disappoint him. I'm nervous because I know he's watching me and I am so afraid that I am going to do something wrong and upset him. I walked on eggshells around him like he was a god or something. I loved my dad but as I recalled this scene in my mind, I understand that my father was broken too. I can see the love and the hurt in his eyes toward my mother. She's not here so he's looking at me to sought of step up to the plate and take care of the house afterall I was the oldest daughter, but I hadn't been taught. Unbeknownst to me at the time, my father was missing my mom and held me to a higher standard than I realized and that he probably should have, considering that I was only a child in need of love myself. So you see, I understand now how love had been misplaced or disgraced, and that I had been somewhat caught up in the middle of it all. It affected me before I understood that it did and it caused me to be crippled in the upbringing of my own kids, another story, but a truth that needs to be shared.

But God put this desire for love in me, why? What was His motive for doing this? What did He want me to learn through all of this? Who was He making me to become and why? I would find out sooner or later. We were not a family that talked about "love". I can never recall my parents saying

"I love you". But here I am now, at a place in my life and the NEED to hear it has grown just like I have. I had no problem throwing myself around to anyone who said that they loved me. Those few words that I had longed to hear my entire life drew my attention to whoever I thought spoke them in sincerity. I didn't just want to be loved, I needed to be loved!!!

You are probably wondering, "Well what does all of this have to do with FAITH?" The Bible tells us in Galatians 5:6, "For in Jesus Christ neither circumcision avails anything, nor uncircumcision; but faith which works by love". "Faith makes a man seek to do the will of Christ; love tells him what that will is" (Ellicott's Commentary for English Readers). This need for love is what drew me to God in the first place. I was looking for love in all the wrong places and finally…I had run out of options. I had nowhere else to turn. Either He would fix my life, or I would take my life. What a demand to place on God!!! Little did I know that this was all a part of the ultimate plan that He had already predestined to take place in my life, so I was really "right on schedule". Because my relationship with my earthly father had been broken, it was hard for me to have faith that my Heavenly Father would provide for me. I knew He could but I did not think He would.

I had placed total trust in my earthly father and I felt that he had let me down. I did not know my Heavenly Father well enough yet so I did not know how to place trust in Him either. Sometimes we have to go back to the basics to discover when our faith was first compromised, this is one of the first steps to rediscovering it again. When was the lie told and why was it so believable? When you learn the truth, that lie goes straight back to the pit of hell where it came from. So be open to the truth that God wants to share with us and stop wanting to be justified in holding on to the lie. I lost a lot of years trying to clean up the lie that was actually hiding the truth that I needed to go forward with my life. I wasted a lot of time, BUT GOD is giving me all those years back that the enemy stole. Due to a lack of understanding then, He has caused me to be completely *HEALED* from past mistakes and past hurts.

As stated, I was very promiscuous due to the overwhelming need for love in my life. I remember standing outside of my grandmother's house one night pleading with her to keep my baby so that I could go out with my friends. Grandma insisted that I stay home with the baby but I wanted to go out. Despite my grandmother screams to make me come back in to get the baby, I walked out of the house. As I stood outside of her window, I could hear the baby crying and grandma trying desperately to calm him down. I began to look up to the sky and I remember saying to God "Lord, I want a change," "I don't want to live like this anymore". As soon as those words hit the air, a good friend of mine drove into the yard. She was saved. She had been visiting her family who lived in the area and was stopping by to see me on her way home. So she drives up and says "Hey girl, what are you doing tonight?" I told her that I had just told the Lord that I was tired of living like this and that I was ready for a change. She said "Well, do you want to be saved?" I said "yeah, I think I do". So she took me down the street to another friends' house who was also saved, and she went over the plan of salvation with me. Now I did not know what being saved was all about, I just knew that I was willing to do anything that was different from what I had been used to. This lady read me the plan of salvation, I accepted it and I tell you it felt so good!!! I did not understand all that had taken place but I do know that I knew that something was different. Could I physically see any changes? No. Did the mess I was in change? No. But something *was* different…I WAS SAVED!!! I was so excited!!! I felt that change had truly come!!!! I started going to church and hanging around people who were saved.

I was listening to the Word of God and studying. I loved to read the Word because I was so interested and wanted to know more about what God had to say about me and my life. I wanted to know more about God Himself and Heaven and the spiritual realm. I began having spiritual dreams. I didn't really understand many of them or much of what I was reading but I enjoyed reading and dreaming because I felt a true connection to God. I learned of Him and I wanted more of Him. For the first time in my life, I felt that I belonged. Like I fit in. Like…I was loved!!!

This NEW LIFE in Christ allowed me to understand a lot of things about faith and about my experiences up to this point. It's almost like the pieces of a puzzle now coming together and you have a clear indication of what the picture will be. My life began to make sense to me as I studied the Word of God. I began to understand love because now I knew that God is Love. I was still having dreams. Some brought understanding, some I'm still seeking clarity on, while others have yet to be fulfilled. I do know however, that I have an adversary, the devil who dispatched demonic forces at an early age in my life to destroy God's plan for me. His mission was to LIE to me and make me believe that his lies were true.

This seemed to be an easy enough task for him considering that I was young, naïve, lacked understanding, and already looking for love. Because I believed satan's lies, I easily mistook abuse for love while being taken advantage of. I had the definition of love so twisted that my behavior was seriously degraded to what I believed love was. I was physically and verbally abused by men and I accepted that behavior because I thought that meant they loved me. But thanks be to God who had already given me the victory over the devil, death, the grave, and hell!!! Who had already declared ME and YOU victorious in Christ Jesus. We may not know right away all of the plans or even the purpose for which we are born, but satan knows. A spiritual war was going on over my soul before I even understood that I was in a battle. Generational curses have to be broken over our lives and the lives of our children. That is why it is insistently urgent that we run to the Lord for wisdom, knowledge, and understanding. Trust, if Satan could have destroyed me, he would have done so a long time ago, but God said "Not So". You can touch whatever you want in her life, but on her life itself, **"DO NOT LAY A FINGER!!!"**

And the Lord said unto Satan (making reference to Job)"
Behold, all that he hath is in thy power;

A Faith That Works

Only upon himself put not forth thine hand".
So Satan went forth from the presence of the Lord
(Job 1:12, KJV).

Satan can only make a suggestion, God will permit some things to happen in our lives, but He is still in complete control of them all. Although God has declared a thing as "True" in our lives as far as purpose is concerned, we still have to "walk that thing out". This journey is not just one of faith, it is one of obedience to God. Why do we obey God? Because we love Him, we believe on Him, we trust in Him, and in His plans for our lives. God assured me again and again that "if I have faith as small as a mustard seed, I can say to any mountain, move from here to there, and it will move. Nothing will be impossible for me" (Matthew 17:20, New International Version). 2 Cor. 1:20 says "For all the promises of God in Him are yea, and in Him Amen, unto the glory of God by us.

Just like it takes a mustard seed of faith to believe God, it also only takes a mustard seed of doubt to prevent His hand from moving!!! Just like faith without works is dead, doubt and unbelief also causes the Word of God to not be active and alive in your life. The Word only comes to life and works for us when it is mixed with faith. What about you? Have you ever experienced something so unsettling that it shook you down to your very core? Maybe it was a dream or some unusual situation? You couldn't call on family or friends, you didn't even know who to tell. All you could do was to cry out and call on the name of Jesus because you knew that He was the ONLY one who could help you in this situation. In the wee hours of the morning I have found myself on my knees crying on my face before the Lord pleading with Him to fix my life, and increase my faith in Him. He was doing it already through what I was experiencing, I just didn't know it!!! He was breaking me!!!

I thank God for leaders who will get out of their beds anytime of morning, noon, or night, and go to bat for you. They will address your needs and concerns, pray with you and seek God with you until you are able to seek Him and stand on your own. They are more than willing to teach you all about spiritual warfare and the spiritual realm and the evil forces of satan. Lord I thank you for leaders who do not sugarcoat the Word of God, but who stand on the truth and live truth before all men!!! Ones who never murmur or complain about your constant nagging or the fact that you just can't seem to pull it together or get it right. I will always have a special place in my heart for my leaders. They didn't throw me away or make a public show of my shortcomings, they walked alongside me and helped me until I got it right and was able to walk on my own. You would think that by now my faith in God would be insurmountable, uhmmm…it wasn't. See even though God has dealt to each of us a measure of faith (Romans 12:3) that measure is often tried, tested, and stretched. God will use a different circumstance or situation to grow our faith and trust in Him. This is only in an effort to keep us humble and seeking His direction with every issue of life. This is where I failed the most. Either I could not believe God for anything or **MY FAITH JUST WASN'T WORKING!** I chose to believe the latter.

Adrian Rogers said it this way;
"A faith that hasn't been tested cannot be trusted".

I KNEW that I was believing God to work on my behalf, but I wasn't receiving what I was believing so my faith was not working (I thought). Now God would give me little miniature victories (if I could call them that) just to let me know that He was hearing my prayers, that He was watching me, and that He has always had my best interest in mind. I sought God often, I fasted, I prayed, but no shift in my circumstances. I did not understand what was happening. I watched as the days, the months, and the years went by, how God responded to and moved for others. He was blessing them, and they were joyously testifying about how God had come through for them. I became angry with God. I developed the thought in my mind that God did not like me (let alone love me) that He could not stand me, that I was filthy, that God was not pleased with my life because of sin, and that no matter how much I prayed, God would not hear me. I made myself believe this and therefore I spiraled into a state of complete isolation from God.

THE MIND...BELIEVING GOD!!!

I remember this commercial that comes across the television screen regularly stating that "A mind is a terrible thing to waste". This is a true statement considering at the time, I was so naïve to many things. The insecurities and the emotional battles I faced about myself and my current state, only made my flesh succumb to what I was thinking. I tell you, the mind is an all- powerful thing. If used improperly or not renewed daily, can have a detrimental effect on your life and your overall mental state. I became frustrated with the process, my lack of progress, and I hated that I wasn't "getting it" like everyone else seemed to be. I began to "purposely" not care about anything, including life. I felt like I was losing my mind. I began to rebel against God, being stubborn, justifying my sins before Him. I was a wretch undone. I weep as I realize how ignorant I was to His grace and mercy and His everlasting love, but He loved me unconditionally, and NEVER wavered. I had no clue how much He thought of me, that He loved me as the apple of His eye and when He looked at me He saw the shed blood of Christ that covered my sins completely. I had read scriptures about having the mind of Christ (Phil. 2:5) and being transformed by the renewing of your mind (Romans 12:2) but I struggled with how to do that. How can I change my own mind? I'm not God. If He doesn't want me to think it, He would take it from me. I wanted to throw everything back on God, but guess what He did? He threw it right back on me and said "NO, I have given YOU the power to tread on serpents and scorpions, and over ALL the power of the enemy: and nothing shall by any means hurt you (Luke 10:19).

Like spoon feeding a baby, I had to eat small portions of the Word until I was able to handle full course meals. My battle was against my own self. After I had lived so long under Satan's authority (in the world) I had to learn (after giving my life to Christ) how to live under His authority (by the Spirit). That meant that my thoughts had to come under subjection and line up with the Word of God. I had to be transformed by the renewing of my mind so that God could give me this new wine. See, there was so much more of Himself that God was trying to pour into me that I could not receive because I was not thinking right. I could not think or see beyond my current circumstances. I tell you the truth, when I made up my mind to see beyond where I was and trust God for greater, I began to experience joy, peace, and understanding. God's love began to fill my heart again. He began to show me who He was on a higher level. So, was faith working? Of course, it was. It was my own mind that I had to bring under subjection to the Word of God. I had to go back and take back every lie that the enemy had told me and cast them down at the foot of Jesus who gave me the TRUTH according to God's Word. For every lie that Satan had told me, I went to the Word of God and found the truth about that thing. After the glorious light of God's grace shined on me, I was ready. Ready to exercise my faith in the promises of God. I went back and I repented before the Lord for being angry at

Him due to my own lack of understanding to what He was doing. I repented for not knowing or understanding His love and His peace that passeth all understanding (Phil. 4:7). I repented for questioning the faith that He'd given me because I did not know how to use it properly. We must realize that we have a thief that comes only to steal, kill, and to destroy our lives (our faith) but God is come that we might have life, and that we may have it more abundantly in its entirety, to the full (John 10:10). We must believe without question that God is who He says He is. We must trust Him fully without allowing our own thoughts to interfere with His ability to provide all that we need. He is an ALL-SUFFICIENT GOD and trusting Him would make our lives so much more rich and substantive.

    FAITH WORKS… NOW WORK YOUR FAITH!!!

Teresa A. Stith

Share a time when you thought that your faith was not working. Why did you feel this way and what changed your perspective on it?

_____

_____

_____

_____

_____

_____

_____

_____

_____

_____

_____

_____

CHAPTER 2

OVERCOMING OBSTACLES

According to the infamous "®Google", an obstacle is a "thing" that blocks one's way or prevents or hinders progress. It's a stumbling block, a hindrance, a handicap, a problem, a disadvantage, or a curb. I included all of these definitions so that you could find yourself in your own struggles and identify exactly where you are in your mess. What has been the one thing that has blocked your path or hindered your progress? Maybe it was a person. It could be a nagging habit or a deep rooted sin. Whatever your battle is, you have to decide that you are ready to face it head on. Many of the challenges to my faith resulted because I did not want to look at certain things about my life. I kept sweeping situations under the rug, telling myself that I would deal with it later and later never came. Some things lay dormant in my heart for years and grew into seeds of bitterness, grudges, and hatred. As God exposed what was really in my heart, I had to decide that I needed His strength to face these things and overcome them. Faith in God gave me the confidence that I needed to endure this process. It was not easy. No one wants to look at their lives and take the blame for it being the way that it is when it is so much easier to shift the blame to someone else. I would not want someone reading this book (if you know me) to feel in any way responsible for what I felt or what I have had to endure. What I went through was exactly what was needed for me to find God in my life. What you go through is what will be needed for you to find God in your life. For this is His will concerning all of us, that we come to know who He is through our sufferings. What God does to get us there is all a part of His design and purpose that has already been planned since before our arrival here. But God made me look at myself. He made me see myself through His eyes and I did not like what I saw.

> *The Lord is not slack concerning His promise,*
> *as some men count slackness; but is longsuffering to*
> *us-ward, not willing that any should perish,*
> *but that all should come to repentance*
> *(2 Peter 3:9).*

Why do we have obstacles? What purpose do they serve? I can tell you that they certainly come to try our faith and in most cases, draw us to a closer relationship with our Lord. They come to "prove" us, to teach us wisdom, and to humble us. The Bible tells us in Deuteronomy 8:2 "And thou shalt remember all the way which the Lord thy God led thee these forty years, in the wilderness to humble thee, and to prove thee, to know what was in thine heart, whether thou wouldest keep His commandments, or no. The first thing that the Lord urges us to do is to "remember". One key to overcoming obstacles and increase in faith is to remember and recall those circumstances that God has already given us victory over. Everyone has faced something that we did not think we would ever get pass. Whether it was a financial hardship, an eviction, repossessions, incarceration, drug addiction, some sexual sin, or life-threatening illness, God gave us everything that we needed to face it and defeat it. Right now, you may be facing a hardship and you do not know what to do to get out of the mess. It seems that when it rains, it pours and all you can do at this point is cry out "Lord help me!!!" "Lord deliver me out of this mess!!!". You have put every scripture that you know on this situation and it still does not seem to be moving. What do you do? I will tell you what to do…You remember God's deliverances and praise your way through it!!! You stand boldly and consistently on the Word of God, and you do it with all of your might!!! Give

God's Words back to Him, He loves when we remind Him of what He says in His Word. He has to respond to your faith!!!

> God would not be God
> if he failed
> in even one of his promises.
> He never has and he never will.
> God is completely sovereign,
> infinite in wisdom,
> and perfect in love.

As I have grown in the Lord, I have mastered overcoming some obstacles. This does not in any way suggest that I will not be tested or tried, for our adversary (satan) never gives up making accusations against us. The bible references him as being an accuser of the brethren because he accuses us day and night before God (Revelation 12:10). I have learned how to apply God's word to my situations, step back, and believe that He already knows about it and is working on my behalf. Isn't God awesome!!! Who wouldn't want to serve a God like ours? Remembering what God has already done in my life reminds me that not only is He the same God, but that He is still the same *faithful* God that He has always been.

Always ready and willing to forgive, plenteous in mercy, and daily loading us with His benefits (Psalm 86: 5). Recalling ALL of His many deliverances helped me to give Him the honor that was due His holy and righteous name. It caused me to change the way that I thought about situations, and it helped me to "Trust the Process".

More often than not, when situations occur, our first mind is to consider what *we* can do to fix it. Then we result to some manmade resolve. It's only after we have exhausted all of our worldly options that we turn to God for help. Why? Why isn't God our first choice? Because we want something tangible that we can see. We only feel confident enough to think that we are progressing if we can SEE with our natural eyes, the results. Remember, faith is the substance of things hoped for, the evidence of things NOT seen physically (Hebrews 11: 1). God wants us to seek shelter under His Almighty wings. To trust in His provision for us. Some of you may be familiar with this phrase….

"He may not come when you want Him, but He's always on time". We have become so accustomed to saying it, but do we believe what we are saying? Well if we KNOW that He is coming and that He will be on time, then we should enter these tests and trials with trust in our hearts and praise on our lips. Let us change the way that we approach these issues. You cannot approach them differently if you are still looking at them the same. We must gird up the loins of our minds and choose to **SEE THINGS DIFFERENTLY BY BELIEVING!!!**

You cannot overcome any obstacle until you have YOU in check. The issue is not with God, the issue is with us and our own refusal to believe that God is bigger than our problems. For me, I knew what God said…I believed that God could do what He said, I just didn't believe that He would do it for me. So, I asked God to give me the faith that I needed to believe Him for what I was asking. I said "Lord, help my unbelief". I was still looking at my life and all the sin that I had done, and allowed satan's lies to cause me to feel unworthy even after Christ told me that He died on the cross to save me and cleanse me from my sins. This is the guilt trip that the enemy inflicts on every born-again believer. I felt that salvation and freedom from sin was too good to be true and that it couldn't possibly be that simple. Let me tell you, if you have struggled in this area, I want to assure you that YOU ARE FORGIVEN and IT IS THAT SIMPLE!!! God has forgiven you, now forgive yourself so that you can enjoy the fullness of this abundant life that God has for you. You will not be able to fully trust God if you do not FULLY believe in His work on the cross. You have been saved, by faith, THROUGH GRACE!!! Accept this free gift of salvation, this freedom in Christ, this NEW WINE, and... LIVE!!!

A MOMENT OF REFLECTION

God has dealt to EVERY MAN a measure of faith however, what you decide to do with your measure can have a great impact on how you view situations and circumstances and how well you are able to overcome obstacles. Although stressful at times, these things come to strengthen our faith and deepen our relationship with the Lord. It is my hope that you will slow down a bit and REFOCUS on why you are here (IN THIS PLACE) in the first place! I hope that you will discover the power of faith that you may reap all the benefits of a Spirit-filled life in Christ. It's not always what it looks like!!! We must REFOCUS, RETHINK, AND REGROUP!!!! Fine tune your happiness by knowing what the Word of God says about your current situation. Why are you here? The bible clearly tells us in Ecclesiastes 3:1...

Teresa A. Stith

"To everything there is a season, and a time to every purpose under the heaven".

Understanding this, we know that at some time on this journey, we are destined to be faced with some unfortunate events that try us down to our very core. Some of these things are not really worth all of the attention that we give to it. As a matter of fact, the more attention we give to a situation that's beyond our control, only increases its control over us. LET IT GO!!! We cannot change one thing about it until we change the way that we see it. Let life run its course, relax, and trust God through your processes. Jesus says in Matthew 11:29, "Take my yoke upon you, and learn of me; for I am meek and lowly in heart: and ye shall find rest unto your souls". We get so bent out of shape with the least little thing that comes to try us because we have gotten comfortable. We have gotten complacent and lazy. We have become selfish. We want what we want and we do not want anyone or anything to disrupt this place of comfort that we're in.

We have become so comfortable that we no longer think that we need God. This is the biggest lie that satan would like for you to believe. We should never become so comfortable in our lives that we think that we don't need

A Faith That Works

God!!! We have allowed ourselves to become attached to so much stuff in the world that our vision of Heaven is blurry. We cannot afford to become distracted. We must maintain clear sight of who God is to us. He is our Great Sufficient One. When we release control of our lives to Him, we don't worry when issues arise because we know that Our REDEEMER lives and He holds the keys to our future. He is our DAILY BREAD, ALL THAT WE NEED AND MORE!!! We can rejoice and be exceeding glad for surely if we say that we trust in the Lord, then we know that He will show up on the scene every time, and just in the nick of time. Try this: Whenever a situation arises, remind yourself that:

- God already knows about it
- He has already made provision for it
- It's only a test
- I'm going to stand firm and believe God until I see it change
- I'm going to praise God consistently through the process

Our attitudes when going through will sometimes determine just how long you may suffer in a thing. Sometimes, it is just meant for you to go through and endure it. God doesn't want us to appear weak when situations come to test our faith. He wants us to walk and act in confidence knowing that He's going to provide whatever is necessary for us to get through it. We shouldn't hang our heads in shame because we think that God should answer according to how we want Him to. He knows what He is doing and He knows why He has allowed this thing to come. Let Him stretch you. Let Him build your faith and confidence in Him. Trust Him, He won't let you down. You will find that as you release your worries, and your fears to God, your trust level will increase. You will come to know that God does what He says. You will learn that His ways are best and you will rely on Him more and more. It will show in the way that you handle situations and your patience will increase. You will begin to tolerate more because God's grace is sufficient for you. What a beautiful thing it is to trust in the Lord!!!

Isaiah 52:7 says "How beautiful upon the mountains are the feet of him that bringeth good tidings, that publisheth peace; that bringeth good tidings of good, that publisheth salvation; that saith unto Zion, Thy God reigneth!!!

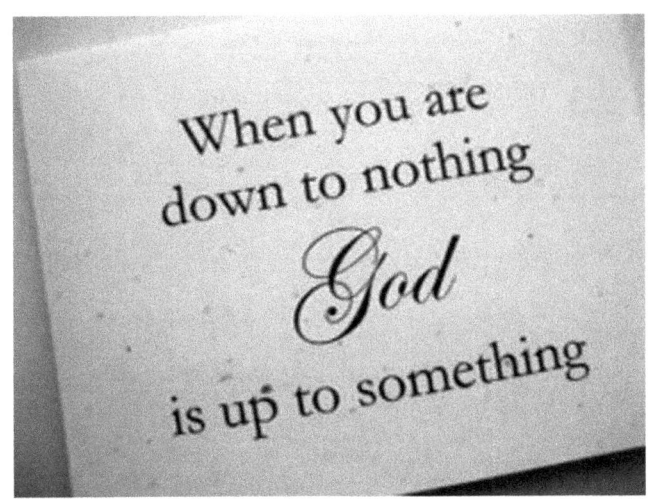

*P*rayer: Lord help us to use our faith to trust in Your great provision. Help us to know that you will never leave us or forsake us. We are the apple of Your eyes and You love us more than life itself. Teach us how to keep our hearts and our minds stayed on You as we see the days becoming evil. The love of many have waxed cold but You Lord fill our hearts with the warmth of Your love. We trust You with our lives and we give You complete control to do with it as You see fit. Perfect us Lord, for it is only in You that we live, move, and have our being. Thank you Lord!!!

What has been the most challenging obstacle you've ever had to face, and how did you overcome it?

_____
_____
_____
_____
_____
_____
_____
_____
_____
_____
_____
_____
_____
_____
_____
_____
_____
_____

CHAPTER 3

LOSING MYSELF

We've all had trials and tribulations that we have had to face in life and overcoming them has not exactly been "the walk in the park" that we would have expected. One of the reasons could be that we have not looked at them properly. When life takes a turn for the worse or some unexpected issue arise, we get all out of sorts. Our first mind is the one that will react first and it's usually in panic and doubt unless we have developed true trust in God's provision for us. If this be the case, then we can through patience, endure our tribulations. We have got to realize that to "lose ourselves" simply means; when nothing else makes sense, when there's no sense of direction, when we know that we are stepping out on absolutely nothing and we take the step anyway. This is a true sign and indication that surely your hope is built on a firm foundation.

"I have been crucified with Christ and I no longer live, but Christ lives in me. The life I now live in the body, I live by

Teresa A. Stith

faith in the Son of God, who loved me and gave himself for me"

Faith only works when we decide to take ourselves out of the equation, step outside of our comfort zones to see what God has in store for us. Have you given God FULL control? Lose yourself!!!

I found this to be very challenging to my faith as I still wanted to control some parts of my life. I thought I deserved to have a say-so in the decision-making processes that were made concerning my life. It was hard for me to move myself out of the way, I just couldn't do it!!! I was curious, yet afraid. My days and nights were filled with tears as I was broken in all areas of my life…in my mind, in my finances, dealing with my children, my circumstances, I suffered on my job, I was mentally and emotionally challenged and drained, I suffered in my body, I wanted to just give up!!! It was too heavy!!! For as long as I could remember, I have always been in control of fixing my own problems, handling my own business, working things out on my own, and making ends meet as best I knew how. Little did I know that everything that worked out, God was somewhere behind the scenes motivating and moving on men hearts to help me, so I wasn't doing anything (on my own)!!! But this independence and control that I had become so confident in had made me so head strong, stubborn, disobedient, rebellious, and unteachable that I did not want to receive instructions from anyone!!! I was such a "know-it- all". If it wasn't something that I had experienced or gathered as a result of my own research, I did not readily receive it. God couldn't pour anything into me!!! I could quote scriptures up and down and I could speak that Word, but I had a very hard time applying those principles to my daily walk. See, I wasn't relying on God's strength, I was relying on the knowledge that I had gained and thought that it alone would save me. Knowledge alone does not save anyone. However, it does allow us to put to work or apply what we've been taught that it may produce fruit in our lives.

For a long time, I used people as a crutch in oppose to really listening to my own heart and obeying what I knew God was moving on me to do. I can honestly admit that I knew (in my heart) what God was saying, but I did not want to accept that it was really Him. Why? Because I was not ready or willing to give up THOSE THINGS that God was asking me to give up. Sometimes I just wasn't sure if it was God, truth is…I did not want to know. The flesh still had control over many of the decisions that I made and over many areas in my life still. I had to be willing (FULLY) to let these things go. Only you know what YOUR THING is!!! What is it that God has asked you to do or to give up? Whatever your thing is, you have to be willing to freely give it up so that you can be useful to the Kingdom of God. The bible says that "No man that warreth entangleth himself with the affairs of this life; that he may please him who hath chosen him to be a soldier (2 Tim. 2:4, KJV). God has chosen each of us for a specific purpose and have equipped us to fight the good fight of faith. We cannot afford to become entangled in this world's affairs for we are on a journey throughout this land. Isn't it amazing that we will ask God to reveal certain truths to us (we already know what the truth is) and when He does, we still won't accept it as being true? I can recall several relationships that I was involved in (for example) and I felt that the other party was not being faithful. I would pray and ask God to reveal anything to me that would confirm my feelings and God was always faithful. I began to see things (certain body language, text messages, private phone calls, hear rumors, etc) and still would not accept the truth after I asked for it!!! I will tell you that in this process, DO NOT second guess what you KNOW your heart is telling you to do. God speaks to everyone differently, but then pretty much the same. In my own opinion, I think that we just hear Him differently. Each one of us have this "knowing" inside of us that is indescribable but confirms that the presence of God is with us and moving on us to make decisions that confirms God's will and the direction that He is trying to take us. We have to be willing to listen and follow the pull, the voice of God. It is such a "Respectful" "Courteous" "Pleasant" "Holy" yet inner sweet unction that you have that is so genuine, it just cannot be described. Oh, how I wish that I could put into words this Holy Ghost that is so present with us, that if we would just come to trust Him and rely on Him, He would share with us all the fulness of Jesus and even give us a deeper insight into who He really is and who we really are. The Holy Ghost is a complete GENTLEMAN!! He will not force Himself into our lives, we have to embrace and welcome His presence. Revelation 3:20 says…

"Behold, I stand at the door, and knock: if any man hear my voice, and open the door, I will come in to him, and I will sup with him, and he with me." Say Yes to God, embrace His presence, trust Him, love on Him …OPEN THE DOOR!!!

Open up yourself, and let the Spirit take control of your person, your thoughts, your being!!! As we let go and fully and completely yield ourselves to Him, our lives will began to be filled with purpose and understanding and joy unspeakable. Nothing in this world matters anymore, only worship, praise, honor and glory to the name of God our Father and our Lord and Savior Jesus Christ. If I wanted to find my life, I had to first be willing to lose it!!! Are you ready to go deeper? Are you ready to lose your life for Christ? Losing yourself is not a physical death of you, but a spiritual one. Let God take you into another realm, another level of wholeness and oneness with Him. Let Him take you into that Holy of Holies place, where the Spirit of the Lord resides.

AN ALTERNATE ROUTE

So here I am driving home one day after a long day at work. I was so tired. I longed to be home in my bed resting. I couldn't seemed to get there fast enough. On my way, there was so much traffic in the road that I became impatient and decided to take an alternate route. I'm not sure how I came to a "Dead End" but here I was. So at this point, I had two options: I could stay here or I could turn around.

Many of us find ourselves at these "dead ends" in life and sadly, many of us choose to stay here, why? There is nothing at all preventing us from turning around and going back the other way, but we won't do it. I will share a testimony with you. I had found myself at a dead end in my life through a relationship that I was involved in. No one had to tell me that it was bad and that I shouldn't have been in it in the first place, but I chose to stay there and deal with the verbal and physical abuse. When I looked at myself, I felt that I lacked all of the things that many of my friends had at the time which were nice cars, a nice home, a good job, and a faithful man (a man period). I wanted to be loved so badly that I was willing to risk my and my children's health and well-being for this worldly pleasure. I knew that my life was going nowhere fast. This guy would come in and find something to argue about just so that he could go off and do his own thing leaving me home crying and oftentimes blaming myself for his rage or unhappiness. I think I stayed in it so long because every day was not bad (I told myself). We did actually enjoy each other sometimes, but when it got bad, it got bad. The police was called many times and even my Pastor came over one day to try to talk some sense into me. All I wanted was what I wanted at the time and no one seemed to understand that or care that I was happy. Lord knows I was so blind. It took me almost losing my life in this same relationship for me to wake up and realize that God did not place anyone in my life that would first come between my relationship with Him, and then treat me like a punching bag and disrespect my children.

Did you know that when you are broken, you attract others who are broken. We both needed healing. Neither of us wanted to genuinely admit that we had errored in the relationship and neither of us wanted to be the first one to end it. We danced around our issues until they could not be overlooked any longer. I was saved still and he was not so every day and every night the Spirit was pulling at my heart to leave, but my flesh was more powerful. Just like the prodigal son, I had come to a place in my life that I felt that I was losing my mind and that it was time for me to return to my Father's house. I remember sitting on the front steps to my house this particular day rocking back and forth and telling myself that if he had come home before I left for work, that one of us would die that day. I had become fed up with my life and the fact that I had let this man ruin (destroy) everything that I had worked my whole life to obtain. Aside from the fact that he was abusive, he had wrecked all of my cars that I had acquired, he cursed me and my kids regularly, and then he stayed out all night whenever he chose. I know that you may ask "why on earth did you stay?" My only reply is that I did not want to be alone. I was broken!!! This was the result of having made Christ Lord over my life and then turning back to the world. There is no justification for anyone allowing another person to treat them this way and still claim love, but I understand those who have done it because I was them at this point in my life. I was broken beyond repair, I had no self-esteem. Even when I heard God speaking to my heart, I did not have the strength to take that step. I kept thinking that I was somehow losing something. This was the first man that I had been with for this long and I really thought I had it going on. I was blind. Satan had blinded my mind and I could not see the reality of where I was, I was living a WHOLE LIE!!! I wondered how long it would be before I found another man, or if I would. I wondered who else would enjoy the pleasure that my flesh felt when I was with him intimately. These thoughts made it hard for me to leave.

Thankfully though, God did not allow things to go down like they were playing out in my mind. Satan had the whole scenario laid out for me about how I would kill this guy and even showed me how I would get the upper hand. I entertained the thoughts to the point of actually imagining myself carrying them out. The truth was that satan was trying to kill me because he knew the plans that God still had for my life, to prosper me and give me hope and a future (Jeremiah 11:29). Sometimes we may veer off on the wrong path, but aren't you so glad that God won't leave you in your mess!!! He knows those that are His and He stands ready, willing, and able to deliver us out of any situation. He did for me what I could not do for myself!!! All I had to do is WANT TO BE DELIVERED!!! So often we talk about the life that we want, but when given the opportunity to change our lives we don't. We choose what has become familiar to us and what we have become comfortable with. Due to my own insecurities, I seemed to always attract these kind of men. Even after I left the relationship I had to pray "Lord change my appetite". Give me new desires Lord, Give me Godly desires. Lord, give me a heart like thine, to make wise decisions, righteous decisions, good decisions. Lord, give me Godly relationships. Send me Godly friends, men and women who love You and who are striving to please You daily. I tell you, though I've been molested and sexually, mentally, and physically abused, I am living the best single life! Until God sends me a man after His own heart, I am content with my life as it is. I love the Lord and I find pleasure in waiting for my husband.

Why settle for the "dead ends" of life when God has provided so many alternate routes for us? We have not because we ask not. And when we ask, we sometimes ask amiss. That means, we ask for something that is outside of God's will for us to have. God is ready and more than willing to give you the desires of your heart. But your desires must line up with what He wants for your life as well. For example, God will not give you someone else's husband!!! God will not go against His own Word. The bottom line is, do you always have to come to a dead end for God to get your attention? You can turn around today. God has made it possible for you to make an alternate choice, to take an alternate route. The Bible tells us that "TODAY" is the day for salvation!!!

Teresa A. Stith

𝓟ray this prayer: Lord Jesus, I get so lost on this journey but I thank you Lord that You are always so near to me and so ready to put me back on the right path. Lord order my steps. Help me to not conform in any way to this world, but be transformed by the renewing of my mind. Lord, I don't always get it right the first time, but I thank you for your love and compassion for me, for your longsuffering and tender mercies. Lord, I choose this day to take the "Alternate Route" that You have made available to me. Help me to stay on course God. I trust You to provide all that I need to remain faithful to You in Jesus name I pray. Amen.

CHAPTER 4

DECIDING TO TRUST

*W*hat is Faith? How do you know if you have it? How can you obtain it? Faith is something so simple that we have made extremely complicated simply because we have not mastered it's application. Applying it could be as simple as "Deciding to Trust" letting go and believing what God has said. It involves pulling your thinking up to a higher level. God says in Ephesians 3:20 (KJV) that He is able to do exceeding abundantly ABOVE all that we are able to ask or think according to the power that is at work in us. What is the power? The power is YOUR FAITH!!! Remember that without faith it is impossible to please the Lord because anyone who comes to Him MUST BELIEVE that He IS and that He is a rewarder of those who diligently seek Him (Hebrews 11:6, KJV).

So then "faith cometh by hearing and hearing by the Word of God (Romans 10:17, KJV).

Rest, knowing that God is working things out for your good. When He is finished, you will be complete and entire lacking nothing. Let patience have her perfect work in you (James 1: 4-8, KJV). Build yourself up on your most holy faith by applying these principles to your daily life.

- Seek God's direction daily
- Pray earnestly to know what God's will is for your life
- Trust Him- God loves when we acknowledge Him and include Him in our busy schedules and….
- Be consistent and persistent in your faith- Things will come to test your faith but you must remain stedfast and unmovable.

I thought that I would have completed this book by now, but it seems as though I have been at a standstill for a moment. I've asked God repeatedly, "Lord, why is it so hard for me to finish this book?" It was almost as if I did not know what to say, or rather that *God had stopped talking!!!* I have been waiting so patiently for Him to speak to me. "Why is He so silent?" I thought, "I am trying to get this done!!!" I certainly could not move if God wasn't talking!!! I felt stuck. Then, all of a sudden one day, maybe two months later while I am standing at my dresser, perming my hair and peering at myself in the mirror, the Lord speaks to me (Smile). It is the most refreshing thing to hear, "that still small voice". I was not so much focused on the message at first as I was the fact that God was communing with me after waiting months to hear from Him. I was savoring all of the juices of this sweet interaction from my God that just captured my whole self. I was in that moment drenched in the sweet aroma of His love to want to share a Word with me. When you have been in this place, you long to resort back here time and time again…in His presence. One thing about the Lord when He speaks is that I hurry to write down what He says because I do not want to miss His precious Words. I breathe in every detail while not wanting to lose what we're sharing. As I turn to grab a pen to jot down what the Spirit is saying, I realize that I still have a hand full of perm that I cannot readily remove so that I can write. By now I'm screaming nooooo!!!! Now I'm upset and my heart is thumping because I'm thinking that I could possibly lose what God just spoke to me. I'm quickly reminded that the Holy Ghost will help me to retain those things that were spoken to me by the Lord, so I finish my hair and continue to listen quietly as the Lord speaks softly to my heart.

*B*efore the Lord spoke to me, I was actually meditating on this chapter and questioning why I could not proceed to go any further. I thought about the title "Deciding to Trust" and the steps that I took to begin my own journey of trusting God for absolutely everything in every area of my life. This is what God said:

> "Deciding to trust is not so much you trusting me to do a thing, the question is and has always been, "Can I trust you?"

I shut down. I wanted to stop listening at this point not because of anything that God had said, but because of my own uncertainties concerning my faithfulness and consistency before God. My convictions ate away at me because I realized that I could be doing more for the body of Christ. God was challenging or calling me to another level of faith in Him and I was asking myself "was I really ready to carry the message that God was asking me to speak?" He wanted me to be accountable. I listened and questioned my own heart before God. I wondered if God could truly trust me to do what He was asking me to do. Why is it that when God is trying to take us deeper in His truths and reveal more of Himself to us, that we start to take our eyes off of Him and look at ourselves to see if we are truly worthy of where God wants to take us as if we need a second opinion!!! Don't you know that if God desires to take you higher in Him that He is going to equip you to go higher? One of the first things that Moses did when God told him that He wanted him to go before Pharaoh and demand him to let the people go, is to find reasons why he thought that he did not qualify to do such a thing. He said "Behold, I am of uncircumcised lips, and how shall Pharaoh hearken unto me?" God assured Moses that He had already taken this into consideration and had a plan for His success. Moses still insisted that God send someone else. God assured Moses that He would be with him. God said "Who gave man his mouth?" Who makes him deaf or mute? Who gives him sight or makes him blind? Is it not I, the Lord? Now go; I will help you speak and will teach you what to say."? (Exodus 4:10-12). Like Moses, we try to hide behind our excuses that we're somehow inadequate and cannot possibly do what God is asking of us. BUT GOD will never send us on a mission without first equipping us for the journey. The TRUTH is that I was not ready to accept this responsibility. I thought I would fail God and I did not want to hurt His heart because of my inability to be faithful or remain stedfast if things got a little heated. In essence, because I couldn't see how God would do this, I too questioned if He had chosen the right person for the mission.

"*D*eciding to trust" had absolutely nothing to do with God's inability to do anything that I asked of Him because I knew that He was fully capable, but it had everything to do with me trusting and believing that He *would* do it. Why do we lack the faith that God is ever present with us? Many of us will keep missing the mark of where we should actually be in life because we are not ready to accept (for whatever reason) God's will. We should glory every time God reveals another one of His promises to us and convicts us concerning our faith. When we come to the "DEAD END" of ourselves and lose all human consciousness to control any parts of our lives, then can we willingly accept the ALTERNATE ROUTE that the Lord has made, living freely and totally controlled by the Spirit of the Living God. Is this hard to imagine? Does it seem a little farfetched? I chose the alternate route which meant that I had to "incline mine ears to hear" what thus said the Lord. I needed to accept God's truths that would ultimately make me free and change my life course forever.

*B*ut why couldn't God trust me? I asked myself this over and over again. What had I done (or not done) that was so bad? Only God could reveal this thing to me. There were many times that He certainly tried, but I always responded like I did this time by shutting down. It was too painful for me to look at myself and accept responsibility for wrong decisions that I had made. I was a person who thought I was "right" about everything. So, seeing the "truth" about how wrong I had been even though it liberated me, it also devastated me (my pride). I had to eventually put my selfish feelings and pride aside and own up to these TRUTHS about my own self, if I wanted God's purpose to be fulfilled in my life. As I laid myself at the Master's feet each day, giving up a little bit of myself, my will, my control…I began to experience the weights that had buried me so far down in debt, doubt, unbelief, guilt, shame, and defeat began to loose their grips on me. I began to experience what true freedom in Christ was like. I will tell you that it is not a feeling, it's an EXPERIENCE!!! The Lord's question "Can I trust you?" found a rather deep place in me that challenged me to the very depth of who I was. For years I had put up this wall, this shield, trying to protect myself and my heart from being hurt, and here comes God (the Master Builder) with all of His wisdom and spoke one Word that exposed ALL my hidden secrets. "Can I trust you?" NOTHING is hidden from Our Lord!!! I thought that I was protecting my heart, that I was somehow still in control of my life, but I quickly reconsidered that thought and began to slowly give myself away. I began to allow God to do the kind of heart surgery that was needed to heal me. I began to release, inhaling and exhaling until I learned to relax. I began to speak God's words out of my mouth until they became embedded in my soul. I began to believe what He said and wouldn't accept anything different. It was an Adam and Eve experience for me.

Remember, after Adam and Eve had partaken of the forbidden fruit, the voice of the Lord God walked in the garden in the cool of the day. Adam and Eve hid themselves from the presence of the Lord among the trees in the garden. God called unto Adam, and said "Where art thou?" Adam said "I heard thy voice in the garden, and I was afraid, because I was naked; and I hid myself. God said to him, "Who told thee that thou wast naked?" (Genesis 3:11, KJV). The presence of the Lord exposes every hidden thing in us. The very best that we can do to hide our sins and secrets from God are not enough, for His voice alone is powerful enough to awake our souls. He knows the very thoughts and intents of our hearts (Jeremiah 17:10). Because He is Omnipresent, we

A Faith That Works

can trust His plans and His purposes to be fulfilled in our lives. We don't have to live a perfect life, we just need to be willing vessels that God can use to carry out His message of love to the world. Have faith in the fact that your steps are already ordered and although there are times that we are delayed on this journey, we are still on time in the eyes of God. Why don't you release all your burdens to the Lord, tell Him about all of your troubles, your struggles. Commit your ways unto Him and trust in Him. Be emptied of life's issues and pressures and be filled with the Holy presence of God, directing you, sustaining you, equipping you, and giving you peace. Don't hold on so tightly to your life that you are not willing to release it to the Lord. Remember, He is our life. We do not have a life outside of Him. Make an honest effort to seek Him and acknowledge Him in all of your ways. He stands ready and willing to lead, guide, and order your steps in Him.

Teresa A. Stith

*"Trust in the Lord with all of thine heart;
and lean not unto thine own understanding.
In all of thy ways acknowledge Him,
and He will direct thy paths".*

WHEN YOU TRUST GOD...YOU WAIT!!!

What are you waiting for the Lord to do for you today? What have you asked God for? Does it seem farfetched? The Bible tells us in Psalms 62:5 to "Wait on the Lord!!!" My soul, wait thou only upon God; for my expectation is from Him!!! Verse 6, He ONLY is my rock and my salvation: He is my defence; I SHALL NOT be moved!!! Sometimes in the process of "Waiting" we have to do just that...WAIT!!! Waiting does not feel good often because in the process of waiting, we find ourselves battling against our own bodies (our flesh), even our own minds, our thoughts. The Bible says to "Let this mind be "in us" that was also in Christ Jesus (Phil. 2:5). This means that even in the process of waiting, we have to think like Christ. What would Jesus do? Jesus (already knowing) that He has victory and power over EVERY situation, was able to live this life and walk this earth (without fear) because of the Promises of the Father, that He will never leave us nor forsake us (Deuteronomy 31:6). God has given us that same power (through Christ's death on the cross) to walk this earth and live this life without fear because WE KNOW that He has ALREADY SUPPLIED ALL that we stand in need of.

We have become so accustomed to "finding our own way" (because God may be taking too long), that we step outside of His will (because we want that "right now" blessing) and end up making a bigger mess than what we started with!!! The Bible tells us that "Now no chastening for the present seemeth to be joyous, but grievous: nevertheless afterward it yieldeth the peaceable fruit of righteousness unto them that are exercised thereby (Heb. 12:11). Sometimes what we are facing may be some chastening that God uses to teach us or bring clarity to a situation. It's something that He wants us to learn, to see, to grasp. Only those, He says, that exercises the full process of waiting or going through the whole situation, will benefit from the blessing that was in it, that will ultimately increase our faith and teach us what to do the next time we are faced with that thing or something similar. So we must let patience (waiting) have it's perfect work in us (James 1:4). Don't tell God you're trusting Him, then you run to the bank for a loan or some man-made resolve. The Bible teaches us to "Look to the hills from whence cometh our help, all of our help comes from the Lord, which made heaven and earth (Psa. 121:1-2).

*N*ow God may use people to bless us, however, the difference is that God is the One who initiates it, NOT US!!! Stop trying to be God by trying to fix your own life....YOU CAN'T DO IT AND IT WON'T WORK!!! Only God can fix your life. If you could do it, Christ's death on the cross would be in vain. I just want to encourage you today that God knows all about it, He knows all about you. He sees you right where you are. He is ready to work on your behalf. He's waiting for you to let go of the wheel and let Him take control. Let Him be God in your life. Move out of His way!!! Take His yoke upon you and learn of Him, for His yoke is easy and His burden is light (Matt. 11:28-30). Relax and WAIT ON THE LORD!!!

*P*ray this prayer: Father forgive me for not trusting You enough to wait on You. I know that only You have the answers to all of life's situations and circumstances. Help me to rejoice in You at all times knowing that You have everything under control and it is working something far greater in my life. Thank you for sending Your Son Jesus Christ to die in my place so that I can now come boldly to

A Faith That Works

Your throne of grace that I might receive mercy and grace to help me in my time of need. Thank you for peace in this situation as I wait on You. I fully trust in Your ability to provide for me. Thank you Lord. 💕

Teresa A. Stith

Can God trust you? How can you be sure?

CHAPTER 5

ACCOUNTABILITY

In my own words, to take accountability of something simply means to take ownership of it, answer for it, or take responsibility for it. I wanted no parts of the accountability process (at first). I did not want to be responsible for anything!!! I wanted to "do me" with absolutely no consequences. I wanted "my cake" and I wanted to eat it all by myself!!! I was so selfish. I did not want to be pulled into the drama that came with being accountable because there were still some parts in me (and others) that had not come fully under subjection to the Spirit of God. There was a war going on in my members and only faith in the blood of Jesus would give me the power I needed to resist the urges and the mind to result back to "my old way of thinking".

Faith is knowing what God has said and acting upon it with no questions!!! Our accountability shows our commitment to God and our willingness to obey Him regardless of our situations or circumstances. Job was a man of great faith who trusted and believed God through all that he suffered. The enemy used those closest to him to criticize him for his faith and even his wife urged him to "curse God and die" (Job 2:9, KJV). Although God was not responding to Job, Job knew that God was still in control of his life and all that was transpiring and that He would answer in His own time. So Job waited on the Lord.

We often lack accountability and responsibility because we are fearful. We do not want to fail. We understand that failing tends to happen but we try very hard not to. As a matter of fact, we try so hard not to fail that "not failing" becomes a battle. It becomes physically and mentally draining. In our own strength, we are nothing. We should realize that we must trust in the Lord continually and earnestly as He has already equipped us with what we need to endure, be successful, and overcome. I have come to know that being accountable to God shows Him just how much I love Him and am willing to obey Him and condition myself to be used for His glory. We have a tendency to over exaggerate and even analyze what God is asking of us. Being accountable did not mean that I would somehow stop living or miss out on some of the things that I enjoyed, it actually meant that I could have all of what I wanted and ALL of what God wanted me to have too, just because I chose to obey Him.

Accountability is "Living Like You Know" and this involves:

- Recalling God's commands
- Renewing your mind or changing the way you think
- Turning to do what God has said

What is it that God has said to you? Have you begun to obey Him? Change the way that you think about what God has said or about your situations in general, then TURN to do what God has instructed. We find this hard to do when we want to satisfy our flesh, but we must be willing to humble ourselves and submit to God's will for our lives. Remember, if we suffer, we shall also reign with Him: If we deny Him, He also will deny us (2 Tim. 2:12, KJV). We must consider our ways by refocusing, prioritizing, and not neglecting the things of God. When we pay attention to what matters to God, He helps us to bring order and substance to our own lives. There are times when things happen that are beyond our control, but having faith in God's plan and being accountable means that we stand firm and take charge. This pleases the Lord when we have the power to take control and we do so knowing that He has our backs. We can release the control we had over our own lives and lay hold to the future that God so desperately wants to give to us. "For I know the thoughts that I think toward you, saith the Lord, thoughts of peace, and not of evil, to give you an expected end. To give you hope and a future (Jeremiah 29:11, KJV). I thank my God for freedom and deliverance from my past. There is nothing back there that I need to move me forward in the Kingdom of God. My lips will speak of all of the testimonies of God and how He was able to keep me and cause me to endure while maintaining my sanity through the process of overcoming obstacles, losing myself, deciding to trust, and being accountable before God even when I thought that faith was not working for me. I'm Free!!!

You have the power to speak life to your dead situations. "If the Son therefore shall make you free, you shall be free indeed" (John 8:36, KJV).

NEW MIND NEW WINE

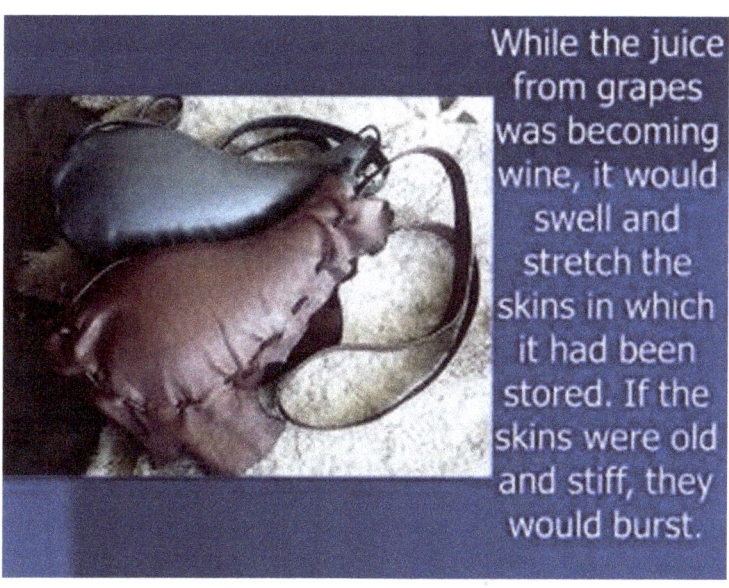

While the juice from grapes was becoming wine, it would swell and stretch the skins in which it had been stored. If the skins were old and stiff, they would burst.

The Lord says in Matthew chapter 9:17 "Neither do men put new wine into old bottles: else the bottles break, and the wine runneth out, and the bottles perish: but they put new wine into new bottles and both are preserved!!! I'll pause right here while you give God the greatest sacrifice of praise!!! I tell you the truth, there IS NO GOD, like OUR GOD!!! God desires to pour Himself into us daily. He wants us to "know the love of Christ, which passeth knowledge, that ye might be filled with all the fulness of God" (Ephesians 3:19). God cannot do this because we lack the mental capacity to obtain what He's trying to give us, meaning...we must change our way of thinking!!! Hebrews 11:6 reads "For he that cometh to God must (first) believe that He is, and (then believe) that He is a rewarder of those who diligently seek Him". How can God fill us with anything if we lack the faith to believe that He can and He will? I allowed the enemy numerous times to trick me into believing that the Promises of God did not include me. I lived beneath my privileges and outside of my rights as a child of God until I began to apply God's truths to my life. When I began to put my faith and trust in the spoken Word of God, the Word began to become alive in me and it began to do what the Bible declared that it would...WORK!!!

Oh that we would incline our ears to wisdom, and apply our hearts to know understanding (Prov.2:2). Our old minds are not equipped to conceive or contain this "new thing" that God is doing. The Word of God does not change so we have to be ready to go where the Spirit is taking us in this season. The only way that we will know what to do and where to go is we have to be sensitive to the leading of the Spirit. We have to be paying attention, and we have to be ready!!! Our affections have to be toward the things of God and our desires have to be His desires for us!!! We must be connected.

*L*et us pray: Father God, we desire so earnestly to receive all that you have for us. Empty us of ourselves and our own selfish desires that we may be found usable in the Kingdom!!! Let us operate with the mind of Christ in its entirety not believing one day and second guessing our faith the next. Let us be like trees, planted by the rivers of water, that bringeth forth our fruit in our right season; that our leaves will not wither and whatever we do in Your name Lord, it will prosper (Psa.1:3). Thank you so much Lord. Amen.

Let the Lord stretch you...If you want new wine,

YOU MUST...CHANGE YOUR MIND!!!

Teresa A. Stith

How Can You Be More Accountable To God?

FAITH IN ACTION

In the King James bible, we learn that faith without works is dead (James 2:18) and it cannot operate alone without works. So what can you do to get your faith up and running? You say "Well I have been believing God for this thing for years now, and it still has not happened" or "I don't ask God for much, but why aren't my prayers answered when I do try to trust God?" There are many "whys" and "why nots" surrounding faith. There are many scenarios that I could give you to help you understand faith, but I believe the root of the problem is knowing exactly where you stand with God? Once you determine that, then you can move forward in praying and seeking God for the things that you desire. When I say "know where you stand with God", I'm asking you "Are you saved?" If you are not saved, God does not even hear your prayers because sin has separated you from God. But let's say that you are saved, you are very active in church and the things of God, but your faith seems to be stagnant. You pray and you think that you're believing God but nothing is happening. Lord what do I do? What am I missing? Have you mixed your faith with works?

I tell you the truth. Some people think that just because they pray and believe God that what they desire will fall out of the sky. That is not exactly how this works. Sure God says "whatsoever ye desire, when ye pray, believe that ye have received them, and ye shall have them" (Mark 11:24) but it's that period when you get off your knees, that the real test of your FAITH begins. This time is really crucial to receiving from God what you've prayed for because this will also determine if you truly believe God, or if you are just saying some flattering words to get God's attention. He knows the difference!!! James also teaches us (James 1:3-4) to "wait on the Lord" and "let patience have her perfect work". We get so excited when we pray that we sometimes feel the urge to help God out by putting our hands in the situation. GOD DOES NOT NEED OUR HELP!!! If you have prayed and released a situation or circumstance to God, that is all you need to do. This too is often why our prayers are held up because we have not totally surrendered them to God. Working your faith, and getting in the Lord's way will produce two totally different outcomes. Faith is an action word and faith moves mountains!!! I have been prophesied to about many things concerning my life over the years. I had found myself praying and always reminding God about different things that people have said to me. I would say "Lord this one said that I would do this" or "this one said that I will do that". Do you want to know what God said? He said "when are you going to stop telling me what other people have said about your life and tell me what do you believe that I can do?" See I used to live off of other people's faith, never learning how to have faith in what I believed God could do. I decided to trust God for myself!!! See God says in Ephesians 3:20 that He is able to do exceeding abundantly ABOVE all that we are able to ask or think, according to the power that works in us (Our Faith)!!!

In the words of Pastor Dennis C. Ruffin, "Are you a Professor of Faith" or Are you a Possessor of Faith?" See people can profess to have faith all day long, but when you possess faith, no matter how rugged the path looks, how dark the clouds become, or how many curve balls are thrown at you....you will plant your feet, gird up the loins of your mind, strap yourself in that armor, and STAND!!! The wind will almost blow you over, but you must refuse to be moved because you know that God is going to show up and show out!!! He will arrive on the scene with Power and Majesty, carrying your blessings with Him. When Jacob wrestled with the angel, he said "I will not let you go unless you bless me" (Genesis 32:26). We need to be just as adamant in our faith that we declare "Lord, I'm not going to let you go until you bless me!!!".

How Can You Put Your Faith Into Action Today?

_____

_____

_____

_____

_____

_____

_____

_____

_____

_____

_____

_____

_____

_____

A Faith That Works

MY TESTIMONY

I cannot tell you when I became broken. I can't recall how it originated. All I know is that at a very young age, I felt the presence of the Lord in my life. I can freely say that now, because my understanding of His presence has been made clear to me. I have always been a person who needed love. I sought for it at an early age. I never knew where the need came from, all I know is that it was there like an itch needing to be scratched. My search for it led me to some strange places and to some people who took my genuine need for it for granted. I was hurt often because I felt that those that I loved should have loved me just as equally, but it did not work that way. I felt that I was dead yet while I lived. I tried to make myself fit into other people's lives. I tried to be noticed. I became promiscuous on purpose just so I could get the attention and love that I so desperately desired. I thought that I was winning in the game, but I was really losing just at a much faster pace.

*A*though I was being loved physically, there was a void…an ache in my heart…some incomplete place in me that no matter what I did, would not heal. I brought this emptiness with me to the altar and although God healed me and filled those void places in me, the journey to wholeness and oneness with Christ has not been an easy path. With tears in my eyes, I will tell you that God stripped me all the way down to my nakedness. He had to remold me and make me over with new eyes and a new way of thinking. He had to form me and reshape me through the storms, the tests, the trials that came to stretch me and caused me to cry out to Him for help. I was pitiful, yet ACCEPTED. I was bruised, yet FAVORED. I was doubtful, yet PROTECTED. I was broken, yet LOVED. Where I lacked understanding, HE TAUGHT ME and when I failed miserably, HE HELPED ME. For the first time in my life, I KNOW that I am His chosen. I no longer have to fit in because I AM IN. The emotional strains that I have had to endure just to keep my sanity at times, have cut me to the very core of who I am. Yet, I stand here JUSTIFIED BY FAITH. I KNOW that my REDEEMER lives!!!

God assured me that I was just as deserving as the next person of His grace and mercy. I thank God for now being in this place. A place of total peace and trust in the Lord. I have no worries about my life or my future because I know who holds my future. God is my Provider, my All-Sufficient God, my Sustainer of Life, He is the Bread of Life. All that I will ever need is in Him. I have faith in the shed blood of Jesus Christ and My Faith is Alive and Active. I no longer have a life because HE IS MY LIFE!!! The word that came to Jeremiah from the Lord: Arise, and go down to the potter's house, and there I will let you hear my words. So I went down to the potter's house, and there he was working at his wheel. And the vessel he was making of clay was spoiled in the potter's hands, and he reworked it into another vessel, as it seemed good to the potter to do (Jeremiah 18:1-4, KJV).

THE END

Teresa A. Stith

FAITH WORKS
SO WORK
YOUR FAITH!!!

A Faith That Works

MY MESSAGE TO YOU ♥

Regardless of where you are on this journey, your faith will be challenged, tested, and tried daily. You have to decide to trust God through all of the issues of life. No one promised us a life without pain or all the riches of the world, but God did say that He wants us to be in health and prosper, as our souls prosper (3 John 1:2). He wants us to learn about Him, serve Him, and love Him. This was the story of my life in regards to finding faith and developing a personal relationship with the Lord. My life was truly a struggle but it was my life. As I reflect, I cannot help but to be grateful to God for keeping me, sustaining me, teaching me, providing for me, and loving me when I could not even do for myself. I blame no one. I accept full responsibility for every part that I played in my own sufferings. All of them was not someone else's fault and those that were, I've learned to forgive and forget. In other words, I LET GO!!! Don't spend a lifetime recalling what someone may have done to hurt you or someone you love. I am not saying not to grieve. Grieving is a natural process that we go through when we lose someone that we love, or something happens that was totally beyond our control. Take all of the time that you need to heal but do not become so lost in the grieving process, that you forget to live your life. I wasted a lot of good years searching for something that was already present with me because I chose to believe satan's lies. Don't let this be you!!! Don't leave issues unresolved or go to bed angry at a friend or loved one. Make things right with them, love them anyhow. I did not know how to ask for help at such an early age, but thank God for mercy and grace. If it had not been for the Lord who was on my side, I cannot begin to tell you where I would be today. God sent me a Pastor and First Lady who spiritually adopted me into their lives, and taught me through the Word and demonstration of Spirit, what true love was. If you are blessed to find such people, hold on to them. The Lord taught me through His word how to have self- control, respect for myself, how to love myself, set goals for myself, and reach my full potential in life by allowing Him to mold me and make me over. He changed the way that I thought about myself and caused me to see my life through His eyes. He made me believe that I was victorious and that there was nothing that I could not achieve. I will tell you that you are special to God and He is concerned about you.

A Faith That Works

It was my struggles though, that caused me to have challenges where my faith was concerned. I had become so used to struggling that I could not grasp the concept that "I didn't have to". When I came to know God, it was hard for me to believe Him for anything because in my life nothing ever worked out!!! It was like pulling teeth to get me to believe that God truly cared about me and what I was experiencing. The lies of satan was so deeply seeded in my mind that God had to do some serious redefining through spiritual application of the Word and totally making me over (heart first)!!! I was broken, SCARRED!!! Like the clay in the hands of the Potter, God reworked me, opened my eyes, and caused my strength to be renewed until He was pleased with what He had wrought.

No matter what your life story is, no matter what your background is, no matter how much you have struggled. However empty you have felt, whatever you've had to do to make your life work, God has seen you!!! He loves you and He is waiting for you to invite Him into your heart so that He can show you His power and change your life. If you are tired of being sick and tired…Give the Lord a chance. Faith works when we give up the control of trying to fix our own lives and submitting ourselves under God's Almighty authority. Ask God to restore unto you THE JOY OF HIS SALVATION and wait as it unfolds right before your eyes!!!

A Faith That Works

SORROW TURNED INTO JOY

We should be so thankful that even with our limited understanding of Who God is, He has promised us a life of absolute peace and unspeakable joy if we put our total trust in Him. God has revealed all that we need to know about Him and His plans for our lives in His Word. We should make an honest effort to know Him, and the power of His resurrection, and the fellowship of His sufferings, being made conformable unto His death (Phillipians 3:10).

We must read and study the Word of God and then conduct ourselves accordingly by getting our houses (our bodies) in order. Jesus revealed to us in John chapter 16: 17-28 that in order for us to experience His joy, He had to go to the Father (He had not been crucified yet). His disciples did not understand this but Jesus explained. He said "you shall weep and lament, but the world may rejoice". "Ye shall be sorrowful, but your sorrow shall be turned to joy!!!!" Has Jesus been so long a time with us and we still have not recognized His presence!!! It is our reasonable service to give back to God what He so graciously has given to us...FREEDOM, LIBERTY, AND JOY!!! Because of His work on the cross, we never have to look at our current situations and be sad, we never have to feel bad because of lack, we never have to settle for less than what we are worth. We can rejoice in knowing that we have absolute FREEDOM in Christ and the pressures of life can burden us no longer. REJOICE!!!

ABOUT THE AUTHOR

Teresa is new to the Author family and writes mostly from a nonfiction standpoint. This is the first of 4 books thus far. Her other titles include *The Real Purpose Behind the Hat: The Broken Leading the Broken, Live Like You Know: Embracing Our Freedom in Christ,* and *Writing About Writing: What Every First Time Writer Should Know.* She writes from a Spiritual Genre and targets any individual whose brokenness has caused them to give up and want to die. She is a motivator, a lifter up of your head, and a strong advocate for teaching, training, and coaching individuals on being the best that they can be. She is the mother of 4 sons: Marqui, KahShadd, DaQuan, and Raquel whom she loves with her whole self for this is where her training began. She has 5 grandchildren whom she absolutely adores. She has a strong compassion for people. She currently holds an Associate's Degree in Criminal Justice and pursuing her Bachelor's Degree in the same field. Visit her website at afaiththatworks.com or email her at afaiththatworks@outlook.com . You can also visit her Facebook Fan Page: Afaiththatworks. There's plenty more to come so please stay tuned. ♥

A Faith That Works

PHOTO CREDITS

Pg. 27- Photo taken from Dawn Klinge's "Look to Jesus"

Pg. 34- Photo taken from "Iliketoquote.com"

Pg. 48- Alternate Route taken from coachellavalley.com

Pg. 65- Accountability taken from partnersinleadership.com

Pg. 67- New mind-photo from slideplayer.com slide 9030800

www.ingramcontent.com/pod-product-compliance
Lightning Source LLC
Chambersburg PA
CBHW062103290426
44110CB00022B/2692